The Thinking TREE

www.DyslexiaGames.com

Dyslexia Games
Friendly Copyright Notice:

The Thinking Tree LLC ● 617 N Swope St. ● Greenfield, IN 46140 ● info@dyslexiagames.com ● 317-622-8852

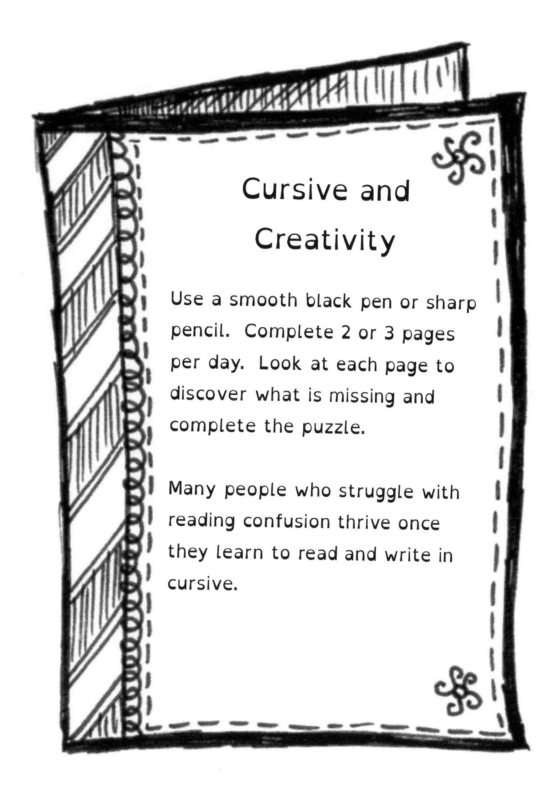

Cursive and Creativity

Use a smooth black pen or sharp pencil. Complete 2 or 3 pages per day. Look at each page to discover what is missing and complete the puzzle.

Many people who struggle with reading confusion thrive once they learn to read and write in cursive.

What is missing? Write or draw the missing parts!

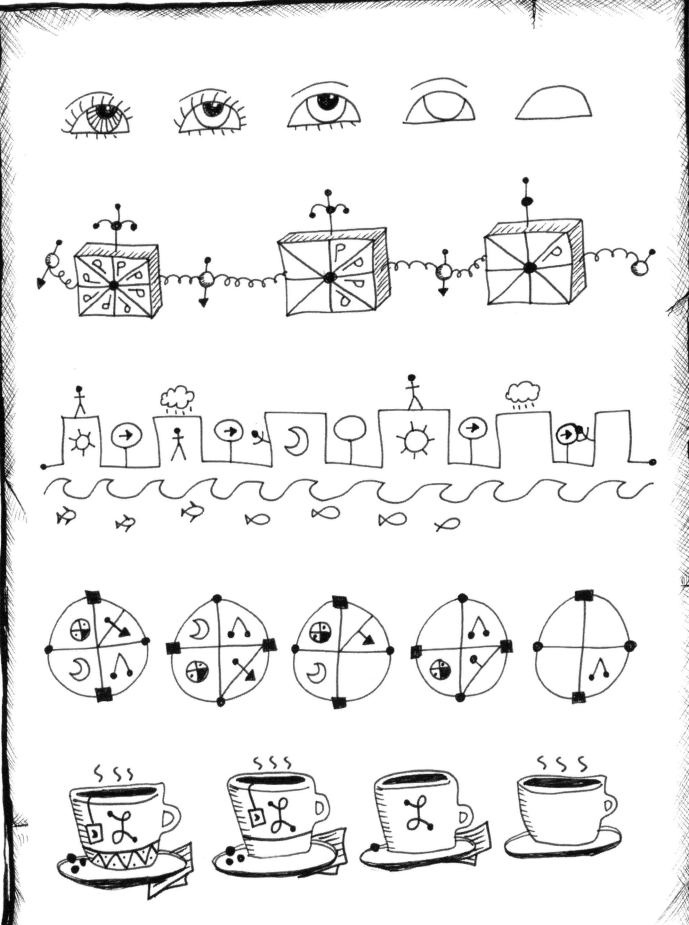

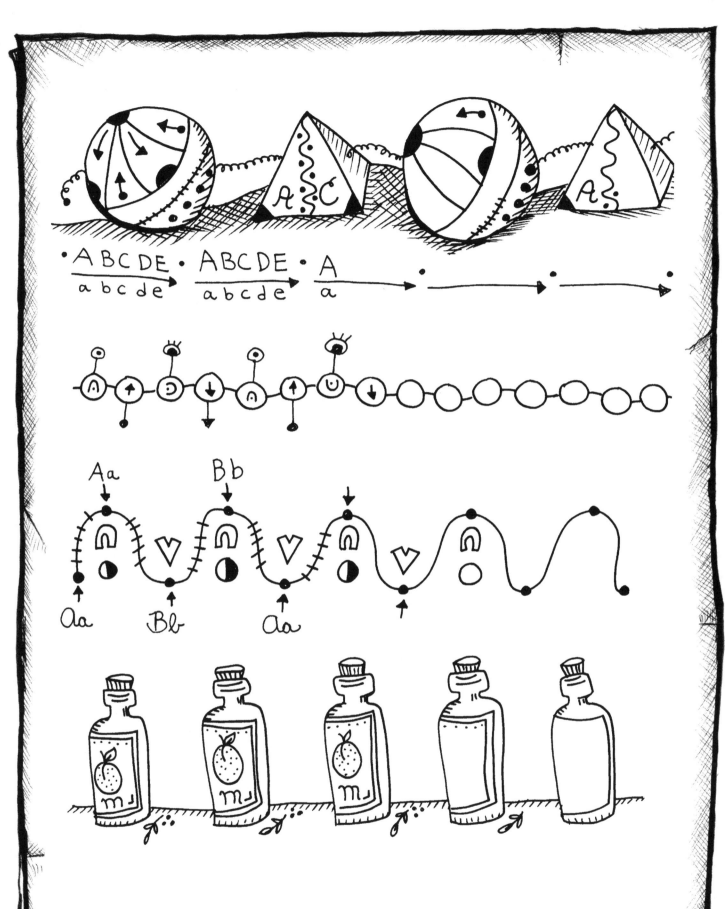

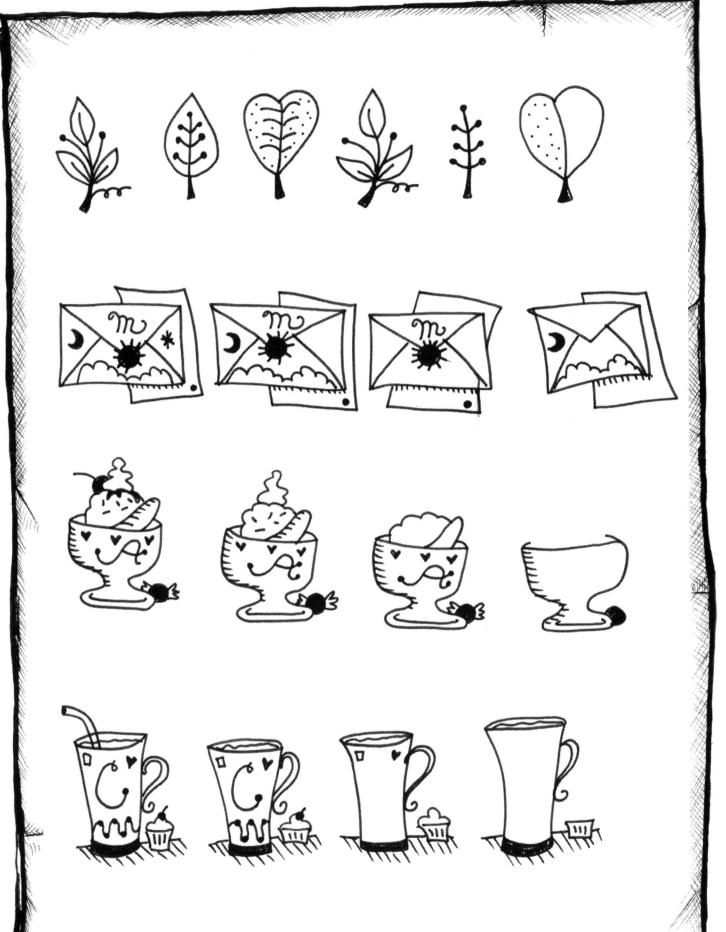

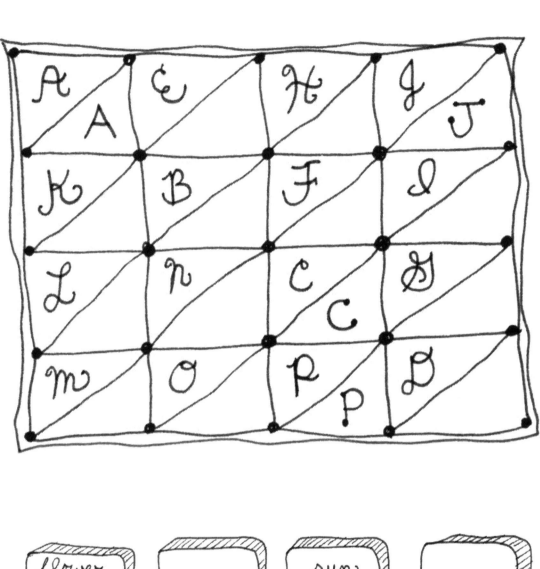

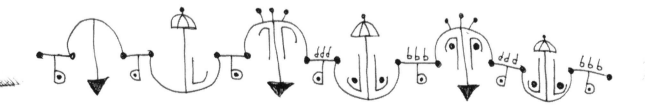

Draw Something!

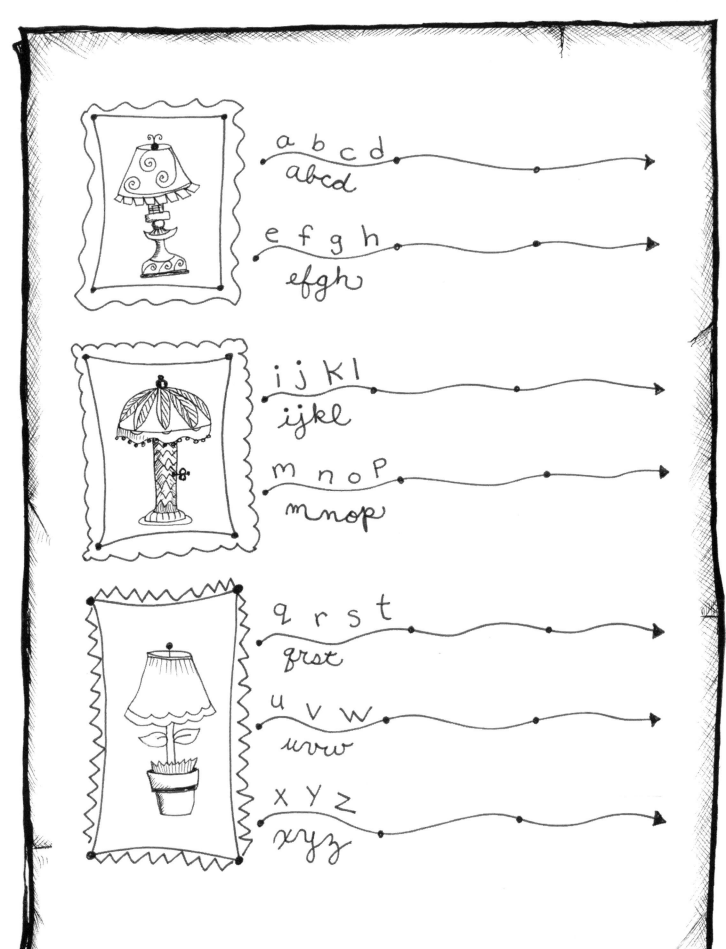

a b c d
abcd

e f g h
efgh

i j k l
ijkl

m n o p
mnop

q r s t
qrst

u v w
uvw

x y z
xyz

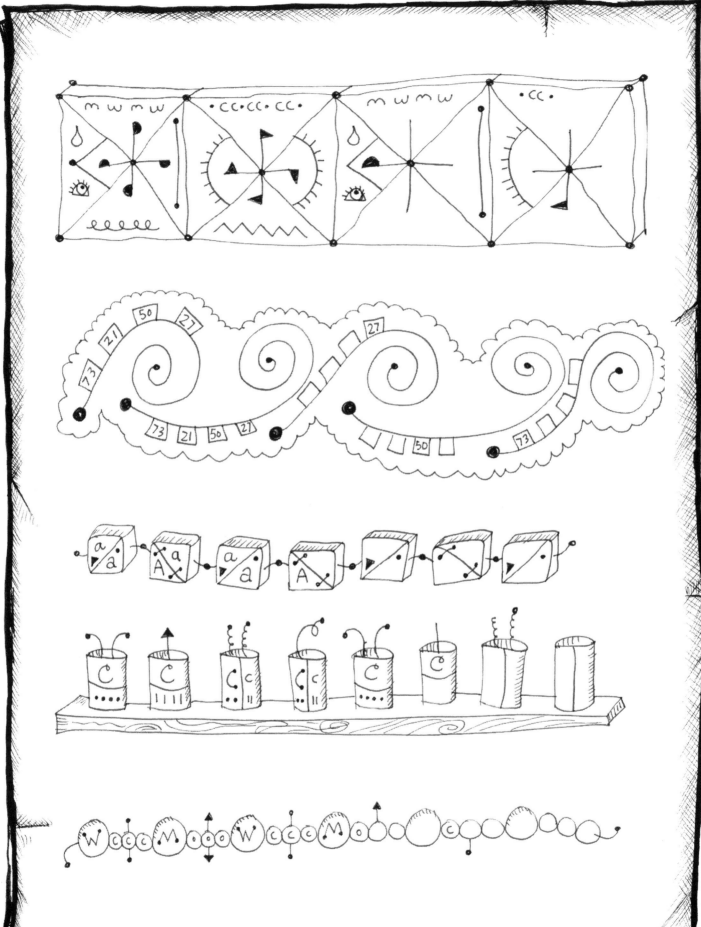

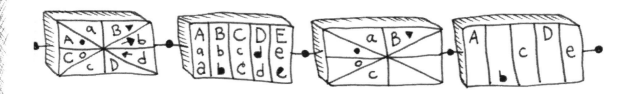

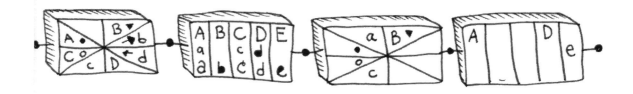

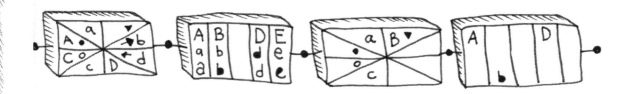

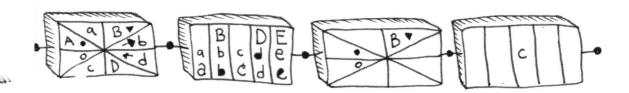

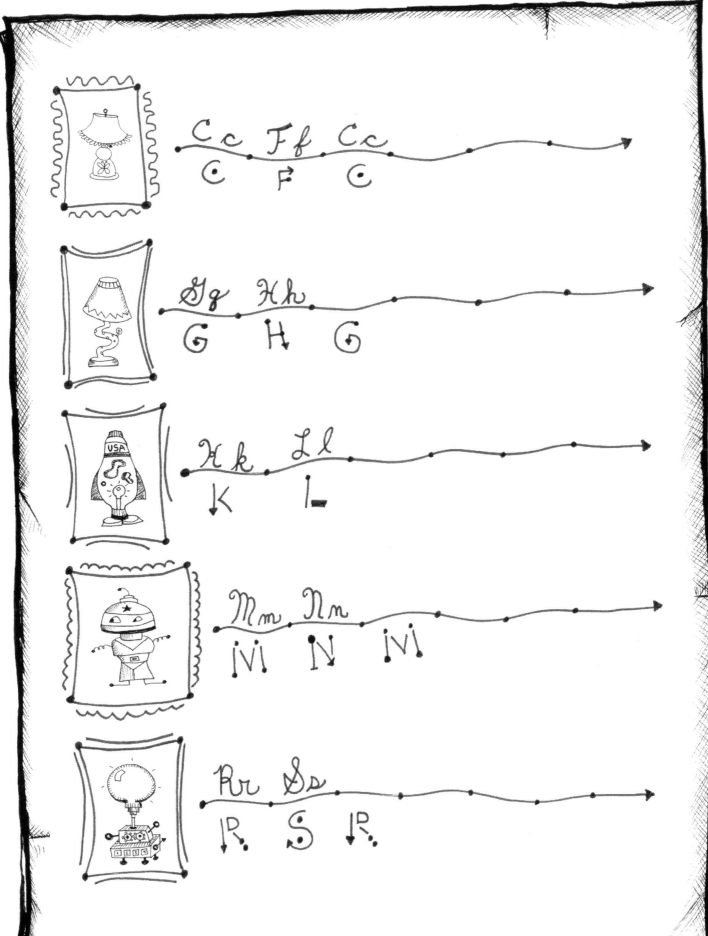

C c   F f   C c
C   F   C

G g   H h
G   H   G

H k   L l
K   L

M m   N n
M   N   M

R r   S s
R   S   R

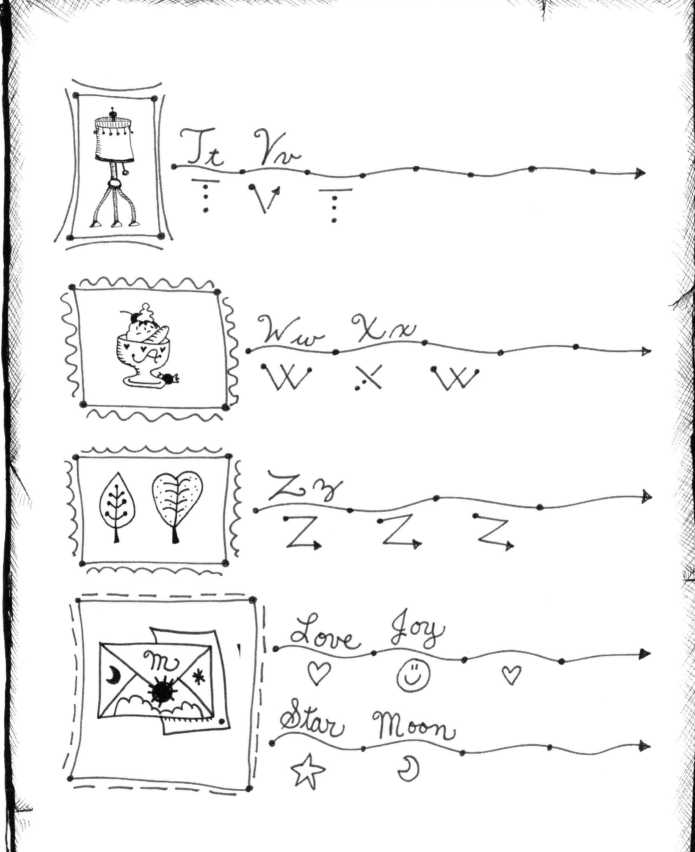

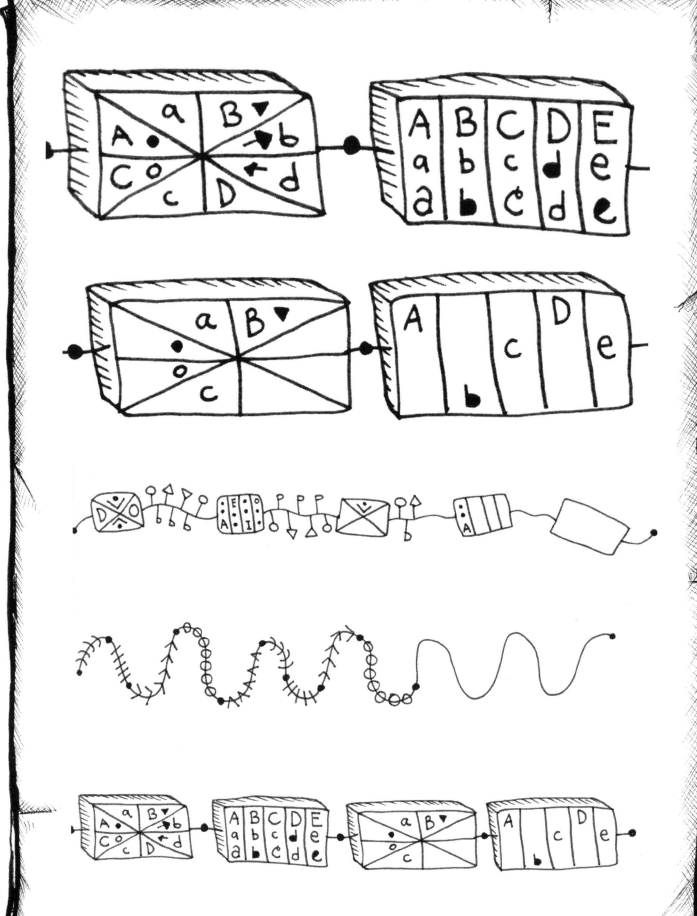

Draw Something!

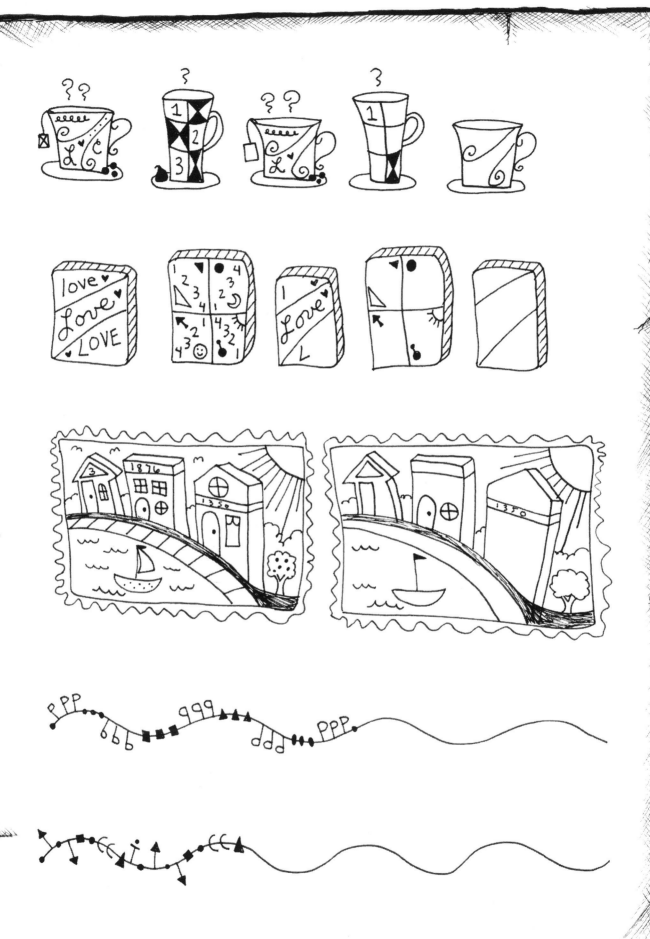

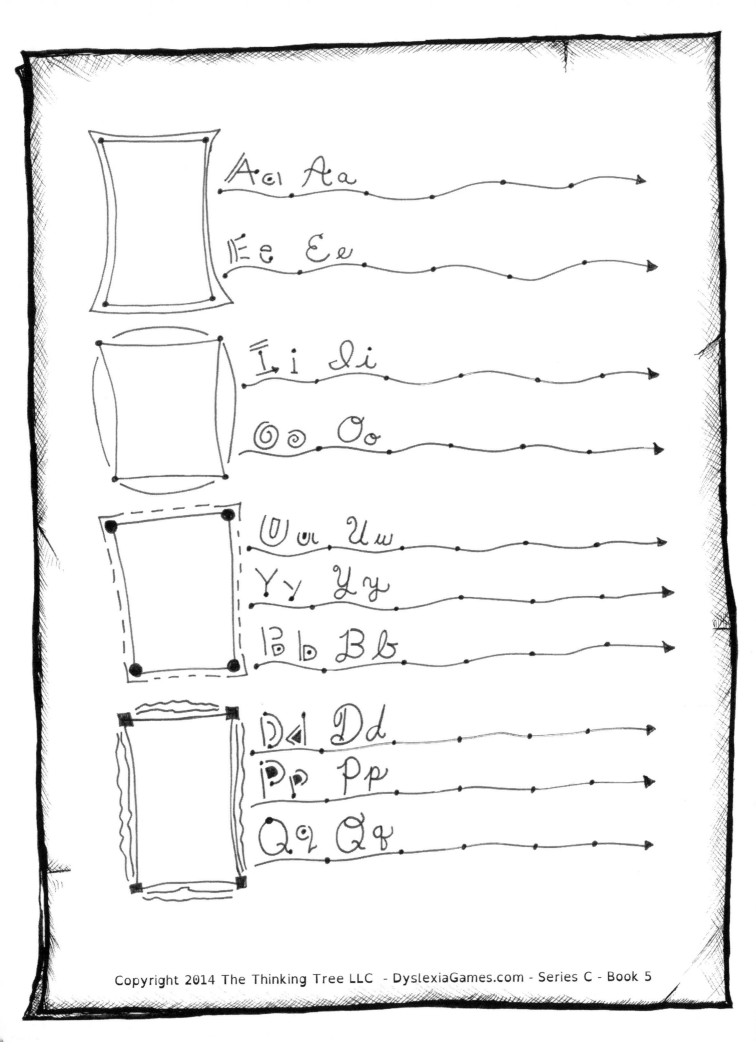

Aa Aa

Ee Ee

Ii Ii

Oo Oo

Uu Uu

Yy Yy

Bb Bb

Dd Dd

Pp Pp

Qq Qq

44604922R00040